FAST TRACK

Fasting To Accelerate Your Breakthrough

*Joe Joe Dawson &
Autumn Dawson*

Print ISBN: 978-1-7350800-6-2
E-Book ISBN: 978-1-7350800-7-9

All Scripture quotations are from The Passion Translation®. Copyright © 2017, 2018 by Passion & Fire Ministries, Inc. Used by permission. All rights reserved. ThePassionTranslation.com.

Scripture taken from the New King James Version®. Copyright © 1982 by Thomas Nelson. Used by permission. All rights reserved.

This book or any portion thereof may not be reproduced or used in any manner whatsoever without the express written permission of the publisher except for the use of brief quotations in a book review or scholarly journal.

Copyright © 2022 | Joe Joe Dawson

Table of Contents

Chapter 1
WHEN YOU FAST 7

Chapter 2
CHANGE YOUR APPETITE 17

Chapter 3
POWER IN PRAYER 25

Chapter 4
ISAIAH 58 35

Chapter 5
THE FAST TRACK (Autumn Dawson) 43

Chapter 6
THOSE WHO FASTED 57

Chapter 7
ACCELERATE YOUR BREAKTHROUGH 69

Chapter 1

WHEN YOU FAST

Have you ever felt stuck? Have you ever been praying and crying out to God, doing everything you know to do but still can't seem to get your breakthrough? Yeah, I have too. Unfortunately, many of us neglect the most powerful and unused weapons we have in the Kingdom: fasting and prayer. The biblical principle of denying our flesh in fasting and prayer can fast track you on your way to your breakthrough.

Sometimes, we fast for numerous reasons. Sometimes, we fast to see our churches, regions, or nations experience revival and awakening. Sometimes we fast because a leader within our church calls a corporate fast. Sometimes we fast just to draw nearer to God. There are many reasons and seasons in which we should fast. However, most people only fast when they desperately need a breakthrough. Fasting and prayer is seen as an SOS or 911 call for many believers. For most it is only done when we have done everything else, we could possible do. Then, when none of that seems to work, we decide to fast. But I want to challenge you with this thought: what would your life look like if you were consistently setting aside time to seek the Lord through fasting and prayer - not just when you felt you were in a spiritual emergency? Generally, we only fast when life is tough, but what if we fasted when everything was going well?

Fasting and prayer are so prominent in the Bible. This is why I am always so shocked when I talk to other Christians who say they have never fasted or even heard a sermon about fasting. The Bible records thirty-five different fasts and four forty-day fasts. As believers, the Bible makes it clear that we are supposed to fast. But scripture really does not put any strict regulations or set specific rules to fasting and prayer. When we read in scripture how fasting helped Jesus, Daniel, Esther, Moses, Elijah, Joshua, and Nehemiah, we should desire that same closeness with God. Reading about the breakthrough that came through these different fasts should make us eager to walk in the same power and confidence that each of these men and women accessed through fasting.

Jesus even made fasting a priority. John 1:1-2 tells us that after He was baptized, the Holy Spirit drove Jesus into the wilderness to fast for forty days. This was the first thing Jesus did after being baptized and before He started His public ministry. Even though He had been officially released by the Father, Jesus still chose to spend a season in fasting before He did anything else. You would think Jesus would have immediately begun to perform miracles, minister to the crowds, and fulfill His Kingdom assignments. Instead, Jesus immediately went on a fast. Why? I believe it is because He knew the power of it. If fasting was this important to Jesus, it should be that much more important to us.

Even though fasting was such an important focus of Jesus' life and ministry, many Christians have been in church their entire lives but have never heard a single sermon on fasting! The church at large does not teach fasting because very few people in modern Christianity actually fast. If we want to walk in the same authority Jesus did then we must do as He did and practice the principles He taught. One of the most vital being fasting and prayer.

Jesus was speaking to His disciples when He said this in Matthew 6:16–18, "When you fast, don't look like those who pretend to be spiritual. They want everyone to know they're fasting, so they appear in public looking miserable, gloomy, and disheveled. Believe me, they've already received their reward in full. When you fast, don't let it be obvious, but instead, wash your face and groom yourself and realize that your Father in the secret place is the one who is watching all that you do in secret and will continue to reward you openly."

In Matthew 6:16, Jesus says, "When you fast…" Take note that He said, "When you fast," not "If you fast." This means that as followers of Jesus, we should fast. Jesus was challenging His disciples to fast and to fast often. Whenever I hear someone say, "Well, I don't know if fasting is necessary. I don't know if it is for me," I immediately think of this scripture. Jesus was very clear when He said to His disciples, "When you fast…" He had an expectation that His followers and disciples would fast. Jesus goes on to say in Matthew 6:16, "When you fast, don't be sad-faced like the hypocrites. For they make their faces unattractive so their fasting is obvious to people. I assure you: They've got their reward!" Jesus is warning His disciples to avoid the trap of wanting their fasting to be seen by others by making their fasting obvious. When we fast, it should not be in order to be seen by others or to make ourselves feel more spiritual. Our motivation to fast should always be to admit our desperate need and desire for more of God.

Several years ago, my wife and I went through a very difficult season. A major transition came into our life and ministry that blindsided us. We unexpectedly found ourselves more dependent on God than ever before. We responded to this challenging season with fasting and prayer. I fasted more than one hundred days throughout that year because I was desperate to hear from God. In the previous season, we hadn't needed to fully rely on God to breakthrough for us. In a way, we thought we were self-sufficient. However, the amount of breakthrough and deliverance we experienced during that season of fasting was astronomical.

In that season of intense fasting, I learned that fasting needed to become a regular part of my lifestyle. I learned to not wait until I needed a breakthrough to fast. I learned to live a lifestyle of fasting. I learned in that season, more than any other, that fasting does not change God, it changes you. Fasting kills the flesh. Fasting humbles and properly aligns us with the Lord. When you spend time with God on a regular basis, you can't help but become humble. You are communicating with the King of the universe. Can you believe the Creator of all Heaven and earth wants to spend time with you daily?

Fasting will shift your mindset and your perspective. Whenever I become frustrated with a situation or an individual, instead of acting out of my frustration, I now respond by going on a fast to get God's perspective. If you will seek Him through fasting, God will reveal His heart and His perspective about whatever is going on in your life.

So, as Jesus said, "When you fast..." set aside time to pray. Take the time that you would spend eating and preparing food to spend that time in prayer instead. Think about the amount of time each day you spend shopping for, preparing and eating food! Whenever you fast you are able to spend a portion of that time, if not all of it, with God. Fasting without prayer is just a diet. Without prayer, fasting will always lack power. Many different religions and cultures practice fasting for different reasons. The difference with us as believers is that when we fast and pray, we unlock the power of God. The combination of prayer and fasting is what draws us to the Lord and invites Heaven to move on our behalf. Fasting should stir in us a desire for more of God and increase our spiritual hunger. We will not experience this if we are simply abstaining from food. The power of fasting is only unleashed with prayer. In fasting you will experience more of the power of God. So, do not fast without prayer!

So, if prayer and fasting is so vital to our walk with God then we need to get in the rhythm of fasting. The best way to do that is to simply choose what kind of fast to go on.

There are many different kinds of fasts you can choose from. You can pick the amount of time and days you want to fast and what to abstain from. However, the traditional definition of fasting means to abstain completely or partially from food. A full fast is not eating or drinking anything. A liquid fast consists of only drinking liquids (mainly water and juices). A Daniel Fast consists of abstaining from meat or sweets and eating only fruits and vegetables. You could also do intermittent fasting. Intermittent fasts are normally a regular act of abstinence, for example, one day a week. This type of fast is a way of integrating the spiritual discipline of fasting into your life on an ongoing basis. A partial fast can mean several different things. For example, you would normally fast from six o'clock in the morning to three o'clock in the afternoon or from sunup to sundown.

Some people eat one meal a day on a partial fast. It really just depends on what the individual feels like the Lord is asking of them. You may abstain from food or make some other sacrifice. You can go on a fast for any number of days: one, three, seven, ten, fourteen, twenty-one, or forty. The options and opportunities to fast are endless. It doesn't matter what kind of fast you do. Just be obedient to the Lord and start to live a lifestyle of fasting. Ask God what kind of fast you should do and start fasting! It's that simple.

There is no wrong reason to fast. Sometimes we will fast for personal reasons; other times, we may fast for corporate breakthrough. Other times, we may fast to intercede for others, for our nation, for our government, or for something specific God lays on our hearts. The point is fasting must become a regular part of our lives as believers. Whatever it looks like for you, make fasting a habit in your life.

The key to living a fasted lifestyle is being intentional. It is easy to fall out of a fasted lifestyle, but if you are intentional, a lifestyle of fasting and prayer is possible. A practical tip for living a fasted lifestyle is to go ahead and plan your next fast before you finish the one you are on. Your greatest breakthrough, or someone else's, could be on the other side of your obedience to fast. Miracles are manifested when we fast. Prayers we have prayed for years are suddenly answered when we seek God in prayer and fasting. Again, fasting is one of the most powerful spiritual weapons we have been given. Don't let this tool go unused in your life! Fasting is a simple way to get on the fast track to breakthrough.

Chapter 2

CHANGE YOUR APPETITE

Have you ever felt dissatisfied in your walk with God? It may be because you are feeding your flesh instead of your spirit. Whatever we feed the most will be what dictates what we will crave. Fasting quiets the desires of our flesh and turns up the volume on the spiritual desires of our spirit. Your spirit is crying out for you to fast. Quit feeding your flesh and instead feed your spirit and watch what happens to your spiritual appetite. Malachi 1:8 says, "'And when you offer the blind as a sacrifice, Is it not evil? And when you offer the lame and sick, Is it not evil? Offer it then to your governor! Would he be pleased with you? Would he accept you favorably?' says the Lord of hosts." What the Lord is highlighting here is that our sacrifices, including our decisions to fast, should cost us something. What He is essentially saying is if it doesn't mean that much to you, it probably doesn't mean that much to Him. When choosing to fast, choose to abstain from something that will deny your flesh and feed your spirit. The important thing to keep in mind when choosing to fast is that your goal is to have more of God and to see Him move. It's important to remember that if the fast doesn't challenge you, it's not much of a fast.

Seasons of fasting and prayer can break compromise off of your life. Many people have up-and-down cycles that they seem unable to break. Fasting doesn't just break these; it destroys them. Fasting can break you out of cycles, strongholds, wrong mindsets, and bondage. If you are serious about breaking out of a cycle, go on a fast. One of the names for the devil is Beelzebub, which means "lord of the flies." The lifespan of a fly is forty days. This is why we see so many examples of forty-day fasts in scripture because forty days can break any cycle of the enemy.

To overcome compromise, you can start by setting your mind to not compromise on your fast. Your flesh will fight you and tell you to quit, but you must fast until your spirit man overcomes your flesh. Psalm 119:9–11 says, "How can a young man cleanse his way? By taking heed according to Your word. With my whole heart I have sought You; Oh, let me not wander from Your commandments! Your word I have hidden in my heart that I might not sin against you."

You can get in a place with God where compromise and comfort zones no longer remain. Remaining in compromise or just hanging out your comfort zone will keep you out of the more God has for you. When you reach the point of no return, you will reach the deeper things of God. I personally encourage you to get to that place as fast as you can by fasting!

Early in my walk with God, I read a book by Lou Engle called "Fast Forward". I was deeply impacted by this book. It stirred my hunger for God and my desire to see Him move in my life and in America. It was in those formative years that I discovered how close we can grow to the Lord if we simply fast and pray. As a fiery twenty-year-old, I would fast several days a week and spend four to six hours a day in prayer. Now many years later, I still treasure those seasons of intense seeking. They are what molded and shaped me as a man of God and as a person of purpose. I read scriptures like Joel 2:12 which says, "'Now, therefore,' says the Lord, 'Turn to Me with all your heart, with fasting, with weeping, and with mourning.'" And I took these kinds of verses to heart. I wanted to give myself completely to God and the purpose He had for my life, and over and over again, I kept finding that the Bible always pointed to fasting and prayer as the way to the more of God.

Still to this day, when my passion for God begins to grow cold, I will go on a fast. When my prayer life starts to get dull, I fast. If I find my hunger for God weakened, I fast. Staying on fire for God takes intentionality and in order to break off complacency, often the only way is through fasting and prayer.

People ask me all the time, "How do I get closer to God?" My answer is always the same, "Fast and pray." Why? Because fasting changes our appetite. And I don't just mean our natural appetite, but also our spiritual appetite. Fasting will make you hungry, in more ways than one! Whenever we fast, our flesh is crucified, we begin to hunger after the things of God and the things of this world become less and less appealing or important to us. Whenever we fast, our awareness of our need for God rises as our spiritual hunger increases. I've never walked away from a fast and not experienced change. I once went on a fast from watching SportsCenter. After a couple of months, my wife asked me when I was going to start watching sports again. I hadn't even realized my fast was over! I had fallen in love with spending time with God instead of spending time watching sports.

Psalm 42:7 says, "Deep calls unto deep at the noise of Your waterfalls; all Your waves and billows have gone over me." When we get hungry for the deep things of God, we begin to experience the deep things of God. Fasting causes us to be hungry for what only God can give to us. During one season of my life, I felt led to go on a forty-day Daniel Fast. Toward the end of the fast, I wanted to extend it. I kept praying and asking the Lord if I could extend it to forty-five days. However, I felt the Lord say no. A week after ending the fast, I felt the release to go on another forty-day Daniel Fast. After I completed the second forty-day fast, I couldn't even drink sweet tea anymore! I am from the South and used to absolutely love sweet tea. However, during my time of fasting, my appetite changed. Fasting changes our physical and spiritual appetites. After times of fasting, we begin to crave the presence and the things of God more than anything else.

We often fast for spiritual reasons, as we should, but fasting also has physical benefits. Dr. Myles Monroe said, "Fasting is God's reset button for the body." This is why there are just as many books written by secular authors about fasting as there are Christian. I have often found that toward the end of a period of fasting, I will have more energy and feel better physically than when I am not fasting. Your body responds to fasting by flushing out toxins and giving your digestive system a much-needed rest. Fasting will change you spiritually, but it will also break unhealthy physical habits. When God introduced the spiritual discipline of fasting, He knew that it would benefit us physically as well as spiritually.

Psalm 34:8 says, "Oh, taste and see that the Lord is good; blessed is the man who trusts in Him!" Once you discover the power in prayer and fasting, your life will be changed forever. Once again, fasting changes our appetites. When we live a fasted lifestyle, we will not be satisfied by the world any longer. When we become truly hungry for more of God, we become desperate and God fills us. Matthew 5:6 says, "Blessed are those who hunger and thirst for righteousness, for they shall be filled." James 4:3 says, "You ask and do not receive, because you ask amiss, that you may spend it on your pleasures." The less we fast, the more we pray out of earthly needs and desires. Fasting aligns us with the heart and will of God and our prayers become more effective. As we deny our flesh through fasting, our desires and appetites shift from the natural to the supernatural. Then we begin to hunger and thirst for righteousness and we are guaranteed to be filled.

Joel 1:14 and 2:15 call us to sanctify ourselves. We do this by fasting. To sanctify means to be set apart, to call something holy. Joel 2:12–19 is a call to repentance. "Now, therefore," says the Lord, "Turn to Me with all your heart, with fasting, with weeping, and with mourning." So rend your heart, and not your garments; return to the Lord your God, for He is gracious and merciful, slow to anger, and of great kindness; and He relents from doing harm...Blow the trumpet in Zion, consecrate a fast, call a sacred assembly; gather the people, sanctify the congregation, assemble the elders, gather the people...Let the priests, who minister to the Lord, weep between the porch and the altar; let them say, "Spare Your people, O Lord, and do not give Your heritage to reproach, that the nations should rule over them." We find a vital spiritual truth in this charge from the prophet Joel, fasting will rend our hearts and lead us into repentance. Fasting will lay us bare before the Lord and then He is able to uproot anything that is not of Him from our hearts. Fasting and prayer will lead us into repentance. It is then from that place of humility and surrender that we come face to face with God. And every encounter we have with God will change our hearts and our appetites.

Chapter 3

POWER IN PRAYER

When I study scripture and read through so many of the stories in the Bible, I see God's heart cry is for us to have a close relationship with Him. When you fast, you draw near to the heart of God. James 4:8 says, "If we draw near to God, then He will draw near to us." This should motivate everyone to seek God daily. From the very beginning, the Father has been crying out for us to come and be close to Him. God came down in the cool of the day to meet with Adam and Eve. He made them His priority. We were made to have a close relationship with the Father and as His children, we shouldn't want just religious programs; we should want God Himself. Fasting will pull us into that kind of closeness with God. It will also awaken our desire to see God manifest His glory, presence, and power in and through our lives.

It's sad, but we are often more disciplined in our flesh than in our spirit. We have more eating habits than fasting habits. What if your measure to your breakthrough and success in life was directly tied to your fasting and prayer life? Fasting helps us return to our first love. We start to focus more on what Heaven is saying versus what's going on in our day-to-day life. Ecclesiastes 10:10 says, "If the ax is dull, and one does not sharpen the edge, then he must use more strength; but wisdom brings success." Far too many people are working hard but wearing themselves down. But if they would fast and seek God, they would find themselves on the fast track with just a few adjustments. We all become dull from time to time. We need to be mature enough to know we need to humble ourselves and fast.

I want to be known as a person with a burning passion for Jesus. If I ever see my emotions or character start to slide, I know I need to fast. As a believer, I never want to get into a religious rut or routine in church. I want to minister out of a fresh encounter with God. I want people to know I've been with Jesus and that His anointing is flowing through me. The more we die to the flesh, the more we will move in the Spirit.

Many years ago, I was spending my daily time with God in the secret place. I asked the Lord to give me one scripture that I could hang onto for the rest of my life. The Lord spoke "Mark 1:35" to me. At the time, I did not know this verse off the top of my head, so I went and looked it up. When I read it, I understood why the Lord spoke this particular verse to me. It says that very early in the morning, before the day had even begun, Jesus Christ would get up to seek the face of His Father. This has become my life verse. Before anybody got up and started asking Jesus questions or anyone was pulling on His anointing, He already had his daily time of devotion with God. He made an effort to get up and seek out a quiet spot away from everybody else so that it was just Him and God. Jesus was very strategic in His prayer life. And we should be too. His prayer life was planned, it was private and it was personal. Jesus had a constant and continual prayer life because His relationship with His Father is where He drew strength from. In a way, Jesus was fasting sleep by choosing to rise early and spend that time in the presence of His Father. Whatever we must do to deny our flesh in fasting will draw us closer to the Lord and we will be changed.

Leonard Ravenhill said, "No man is greater than his prayer life!" This is a very powerful and true statement. The more time you spend with God, the more you learn about His characteristics, and the more you will start to grow in His likeness. One of the most important keys of any relationship is making daily regular ongoing communication a priority. It is only through that kind of consistency that creates a strong, lasting relationship where both parties can flourish. It is the exact same way in our relationship with God. Consistency is key. As the perfect example, Jesus was constantly making time to pull away to commune with the Father. Mark 1:35 says this about Jesus, "Now in the morning, having risen a long while before daylight, He went out and departed to a solitary place; and there He prayed." In Mark 6:46 we see Jesus pulling away to pray again, "Immediately He made His disciples get into the boat and go before Him to the other side, to Bethsaida, while He sent the multitude away. And when He had sent them away, He departed to the mountain to pray." No matter how busy Jesus was, the gospels point out that He always made time for prayer both in the morning and at night. 1Thessalonians 5:17 says, "Pray without ceasing." Jesus lived by this scripture and so should we. I stop and spend time with the Lord at numerous times throughout the day for various lengths of time. When you cultivate a lifestyle of prayer, it's not just about having a set prayer time alone but also about maintaining a constant, ongoing dialogue with the Lord throughout the day. When we seek the Lord in the place of prayer, our communication with Him becomes deeper and more consistent. We all find ourselves in different seasons neglecting the place of prayer. One of the easiest ways to reset your prayer life is to go on a fast.

In Mark 9, a man brought his son to the disciples to be healed because he suffered from seizures and had a mute spirit. The disciples prayed, laid hands on him, and probably sprinkled oil on the man's son, but nothing happened. When Jesus arrived on the scene, He asked what was going on. When they shared the situation, He spoke a few words, and the boy was healed immediately. Later that night, the disciples asked Jesus how He could do these signs, wonders, and miracles so easily. Mark 9:28–29 says, "And when He had come into the house, His disciples asked Him privately, 'Why could we not cast it out?' So He said to them, 'This kind can come out by nothing but prayer and fasting.'" Like E. M. Bounds said, "Much prayer much power; no prayer no power." We must pray on purpose.

We are called by God to live a life of prayer and fasting. In Luke 11, when Jesus was talking to His disciples, He said, "When you pray, pray like this." It wasn't "if you pray" but "when you pray." The disciples noticed that Jesus lived an extreme life of prayer and was in constant communication with God. The disciples made an important connection between Jesus's relationship with God and the power that He walked in. Like Jesus, we too are called to walk in great power and authority given to us from Heaven as a result of cultivating a meaningful, intimate relationship with and connection to God. The three keys of breakthrough are prayer, fasting, and giving. You will find in scripture that Jesus says, "When you fast…," "When you give…," and "When you pray…" He does not say, "If you fast…," "If you give…," or "If you pray…" No, he says "when". If Jesus said it, then each of these should be regular, if not daily, practices in our walk with God.

Jeremiah 29:12–13 says, "Then you will call upon me and go and pray to me, and I will listen to you. And you will seek me and find me, when you search for me with all of your heart." The Lord is saying that when you call upon Him, He will be there, listening. God is a great Father who always listens to His children when they communicate with Him. The Lord says when you seek after Him, you will find Him when you search for Him with all of your heart—spirit, mind, and emotion. In the Bible, the word heart is divided into two elements: the spirit and the soul. The soul is also divided into two parts: the mind and the emotions. When we fix our spirit, mind, and emotions upon the things of the Lord, His Holy Spirit promises to guide us and lead us into all truth and understanding in every situation (John 14:26; 16:13). Matthew 6:33 says, "Seek first the Kingdom of God and his righteousness, and all these things shall be added unto you." The most important thing we can do is seek the Lord daily, building and strengthening our relationship with Him. Again, the most important thing we will ever do is keep a consistent, private, secret place of prayer time with God. We absolutely must remain steadfast in Christ and become students of His Word.

Fasting brings our hearts to a place of righteousness and desperation for God. Through this, we become stronger and stronger. Job 17:9 says, "Yet the righteous will hold to his way, and he who has clean hands will be stronger and stronger." When we fast, we become stronger and stronger. Humility is one of the key results of fasting. In a way, our obedience to fast admits to God that we want to humble ourselves before Him. If we are full of pride, religion, or legalism, you will not see or carry great breakthrough. Humble hearts who call upon God will find the fast track to breakthrough. Again, we never fast to change God, because He can't change. We fast in order to be changed. Fasting does not make us look good before God and we cannot use fasting to manipulate Him. Instead, when we fast, we are showing our fierce love, devotion and dependence on God.

One of the most important things we must learn about fasting is that when we fast the freedom and deliverance, we experience are not only for ourselves. Fasting also makes us carriers of freedom and breakthrough. In Matthew 17, we see the disciples of Jesus trying to cast out a demon from a little boy who kept having seizures. The little boy would throw himself into the fire and the water, but the disciples could not set him free. Jesus healed and delivered the little boy with ease, but His disciples were frustrated. The disciples had used the same words Jesus used and had been given authority when He sent them out, so they asked Jesus why they could not cast out the demon from the boy. Jesus replied in Matthew 17:21, "This kind does not go out except by prayer and fasting." Fasting and prayer was the one-two punch of Jesus. There are some matters in the spiritual realm that can only be dealt with by being a person of fasting and prayer. Why is this? Because fasting breaks strongholds and releases the power of God to destroy demonic bondage. The disciples were looking for power to come from the right words or even just from the authority that Jesus had given to them. However, the power needed to see the boy delivered could only come through prayer and fasting. Prayer and fasting are a deadly combination against the devil.

There are some battles passive Christianity won't win, and religion will never defeat the plans of the enemy. When we fast, three things arise to a greater level in our lives: our authority, our faith, and our power in God. The enemy knows the power of prayer and fasting. This is why he will throw anything our way in order to keep us from fasting and out of the place of prayer. The enemy will often tempt us to feed our flesh and give into its desires. However, if we will simply say yes to fasting, we will see the enemy defeated in our lives and in the lives of others.

Chapter 4

ISAIAH 58

Isaiah 58 is known as the fasting passage. If you've ever read or heard any teaching on fasting, this passage has definitely been referenced. If we are going to broaden our revelation on fasting, we, of course, must also take a look at Isaiah 58 and unpack everything it has to say. Isaiah 58:6-9 says, ""Is this not the fast that I have chosen: to loose the bonds of wickedness, to undo the heavy burdens, to let the oppressed go free, and that you break every yoke? Is it not to share your bread with the hungry, And that you bring to your house the poor who are cast out; When you see the naked, that you cover him, And not hide yourself from your own flesh? Then your light shall break forth like the morning, your healing shall spring forth speedily, and your righteousness shall go before you; The glory of the Lord shall be your rear guard. Then you shall call, and the Lord will answer; You shall cry, and He will say, 'Here I am.'""

Wow! There is so much to unpack in these few scriptures about fasting. First look at verse 6 where the Lord says to Isaiah, "Is this not the fast that I have chosen: To loose the bonds of wickedness, to undo the heavy burdens, to let the oppressed go free, and that you break every yoke?" What a word! If that doesn't get you excited about fasting then you may need to read it again! True fasting will bring us and others into freedom. When we fast, we unlock the power of God to break out of sin cycles, spiritual holding patterns, to be released from heavy burdens, ushered into freedom and delivered from any yokes!

This scripture very simply describes 4 things we can expect whenever we fast. The first is that through fasting bonds of wickedness are loosed. A bond of wickedness can be anything that has a stronghold in your life that is unpleasing to the Lord. If someone is bound it means that their hands are tied. It is the same way in the spirit. If you are bound spiritually it means that your spiritual hands are tied; meaning the enemy is using whatever stronghold he has to keep you from being able to do what God has called you to do. However, when we fast anything that has us bound will be loosed. As we fast and bonds of wickedness are loosed from our lives then we are set free and the enemy is now bound instead of us!

Isaiah 58:6 also tells us that we can expect heavy burdens to be undone as we fast. In my many years of ministry, I've often encountered well-meaning people who genuinely love God that are weighed down by their past. You are not meant to carry the weight of your past. If you find yourself constantly stuck because of something that happened to you or a situation that disappointed you from long ago you are carrying a heavy burden that God does not want you to carry! Tap into the power of fasting that can undo those heavy burdens.

Whenever we fast, we are able to hear God more clearly because our flesh has been quieted and our spirit is being nourished. Because of this, the Lord will be able to easily reveal to us whatever heavy burdens we may be carrying. God deals with our hearts more openly in fasting because we have become tender and more aware of Him. Then, the Lord begins to deal with things that have been holding us back. There have been several instances where I have been fasting and the Lord has highlighted unforgiveness or offense I had been hanging onto that I was completely unaware of. Whether we realize it or not, we each carry heavy burdens. We are often unknowingly weighed down by these until the Lord reveals them to us in a time of fasting.

If you have been struggling with the same issue over and over again or have found yourself constantly falling to the same sin or temptation, fasting is your fast track to breakthrough and freedom! I've encountered many sons and daughters of God who are just one fast away from being completely and totally free. Some of you would not even recognize yourself or what your life would look like if you truly tapped into the freedom made available to you through fasting and prayer.

We see in Isaiah 58:6 that there is a specific kind of freedom that is made available to us while fasting. Not only are bonds of wickedness loosed and heavy burdens lifted but the oppressed go free and every yoke is broken when we fast. A yoke is a farm tool that is placed around an animal's neck that ties them to something. So, a yoke is anything that you are tied to. When they would yoke two animals together, the weaker animal would set the pace and hold the stronger animal back from their full potential. What things are you yoked to that are not from God that may be holding you back from all that He has for you? If a yoke is ever broken off of an animal, it immediately takes off running for freedom. This is a perfect picture of why fasting can be such a powerful weapon in the life of every believer. Fasting will lift the oppression of the enemy and destroy any yoke he may have placed on you. Many times on a fast, I often write in my journal, "God, I've never felt so free! I've never felt so light!" This is because fasting releases us into new levels of freedom as bondage, heavy burdens and oppression lose their footholds in our lives. I guarantee you that fasting can and will destroy those yokes in your life and you will be able to run full throttle after your destiny because you are no longer weighed down by your past.

Isaiah 58:6 also says that fasting will "let the oppressed go free". Fasting not only can bring us into new levels of freedom but it also makes us carriers of freedom. As we discussed in a previous chapter, the boy in Matthew 17 needed freedom from the demonic oppression in his life. The disciples were unable to cast out the demon and became frustrated when Jesus easily set the boy free. They asked Him 'Why could we not cast it out?' and Jesus simply replied, 'This kind can come out by nothing but prayer and fasting.'" If we want to be able to deliver others from the oppression of the enemy, we must commit ourselves to a lifestyle of fasting and prayer. As a follower of Jesus, we never know when God will want to use us to bring freedom to someone else and fasting keeps us in the proper position to release the power of God into others' situations and circumstances.

Isaiah 58:7 points to how when we fast it can be beneficial to others. It says, "Is it not to share your bread with the hungry, And that you bring to your house the poor who are cast out; When you see the naked, that you cover him, And not hide yourself from your own flesh?" Obviously, this is discussing how we can literally give to others the things we are abstaining from as we fast. However, I believe what the Lord is alluding to in this particular verse is how the breakthrough and freedom we experience in fasting is never only about us. Anything God does in our lives is meant to not only bless us but to make us a blessing. I know that is a little bit of a religious cliche but it is true. God wants to and does bless you simply because He loves you. He also blesses us and brings us into freedom so that we can help those He puts within our sphere of influence. This is why I can get irritated with the belief that God wants us all broke, sick and tired. "Woe as me" Christianity will never bring the kind of freedom to others that Jesus was constantly portraying in His ministry. Everywhere Jesus went He blessed others with His words, by healing them, by setting them free from demonic oppression and bondage and by giving His disciples the authority to do even greater works than He did.

Verses 8 and 9 in Isaiah 58 illustrate just how glorious walking in the breakthrough that follows fasting and prayer can be. Isaiah 58:8-9 says, "Then your light shall break forth like the morning, your healing shall spring forth speedily, and your righteousness shall go before you; The glory of the Lord shall be your rear guard. Then you shall call, and the Lord will answer; You shall cry, and He will say, 'Here I am.'" Fasting will thrust you into the fullness of all God has for you. I absolutely love that the Lord told Isaiah that when you fast like I have called you to then you will walk in freedom and give freedom to others. Then, He gives this breathtaking picture of what that freedom and breakthrough will look like. Those who live a lifestyle of fasting and prayer will experience the glory of God described in these verses. Whenever we set ourselves apart to the Lord in this way, we will see His radiant light shine in and through our lives. We will experience healing in our minds, emotions, and in our bodies as we say yes to fasting. Fasting causes us to walk in righteousness and in the glory of God. The favor of God will rest upon us and He will draw near to us as we seek Him in fasting and prayer. Verse 9 ends with God promising that when those who are in fasting and prayer cry out, He will respond! As Jeremiah 33:3 says, "Call to Me, and I will answer you, and show you great and mighty things, which you do not know.'" If you are hungry to hear the Lord more clearly, go on a fast! I've found myself in many seasons where I depended on hearing a word from God to sustain me. When I chose to fast and pray in those seasons, the Lord always spoke so clearly to me and I could sense His tangible presence drawing near. If you take nothing else away from this book, I hope Isaiah 58:6-9 has revealed to you just how much freedom and breakthrough is available to you in prayer and fasting. If you want to unlock the power of God in your life, choose to fast the fast God has chosen for you and watch as you are propelled into freedom and accelerated into your breakthrough.

Chapter 5

THE FAST TRACK
Autumn Dawson

Does anyone reading this love to wait forever for something? How many of you want to wait and wait and wait for God to break through in your life? I would guess none of you do! I certainly don't! By nature I am accomplishment driven. I am a multitasker, shortcut finder, get-it-done kind of person. If I can figure out a way to make something more efficient or take less time then I will do it!

A few years ago, our grocery store started offering a free service called "grocery pick-up". This revolutionized the way I buy groceries for our family. I used to have to take several hours, several times a week to go to the grocery store, put everything in my shopping cart, check-out and then still have to load and unload the groceries when I arrived home. However, with grocery pick-up what used to take me hours and time away from my work and family now takes me minutes! I can now sit on my couch, drink a cup of coffee, and get all of my grocery shopping done from an app on my phone in about fifteen minutes. Then, when my groceries are ready, all I have to do is pull up, and the nice workers load—yes, load!—my groceries in my car and all I have to do is unload them when I get home. That is called fast track grocery shopping. Around the same time I started using this grocery pickup, Joe and I were in the process of seeking the Lord about how to move forward in many different areas, including with our church, ROAR Church Texarkana that we lead and steward together.

As we were praying, The Lord spoke this to me, "I want to put you on a fast track for breakthrough." When the Lord said this to me, my immediate response was, "Yes, Lord, whatever it is or whatever you need me to do I want to be on that fast track to my breakthrough!" Then the Lord said this, "Fasting will put you on a fast track to breakthrough." The Lord was showing me that each of us can accelerate the breakthrough we are asking Him for by seeking Him in prayer and fasting. As God kept speaking to me about fasting, we encouraged our leaders and church family to join us on a fast believing it would accelerate our breakthrough. During that season of fasting, we experienced great acceleration as a community with many receiving breakthroughs as we prayed and fasted together.

So, if fasting accelerates our breakthrough, how do we get on that fast track? It's simple. Fasting is simply abstaining from food and telling our flesh no. Fasting is a spiritual discipline that helps us to say no to a legitimate desire, such as food, in order to practice self-control. When I think about self-control, I think about the delicious smell of my mother's homemade biscuits fresh out of the oven. I don't typically eat bread or feel tempted to eat it. But when I smell my mother's biscuits, hot and ready to eat, I am tempted every time! Each time, I could easily make an excuse for myself and give in. However, I have decided to tell myself no. This reminds me of the story of Jacob and Esau in Genesis 25. Verses 29-33 tell us that Esau, the first-born son to Isaac came in from the field and was very hungry. He was so hungry in fact that he was willing to sell his birthright—all his rights as the firstborn—for a bowl of lentil stew! Esau was tired, and the stew Jacob was cooking was hot, ready and convenient. What if Esau would have told himself no? I wonder what would have been different about Esau's life if he had simply had some self-control that afternoon. Like Esau, when we are out of the practice of telling ourselves no, it makes us more susceptible to temptation. Then the enemy can get us off track. Don't sell your birthright for a bowl of stew! Learn to tell your flesh no. The best way we can do this is to live lives that have a rhythm of fasting and prayer. When we live that kind of fasted lifestyle it establishes discipline and self-control in us.

I love what Joe always says about fasting. "Fasting does not change God. It doesn't twist His arm. Fasting changes us." Sometimes we think we know what we need when God actually knows what we need. We need His presence, His provision, and His heart. God will use fasting, something that seems so unconventional and simple as abstaining from food, to draw us closer to Him. God could have chosen anything to draw us closer to Him but He chose food. God understands the power of telling our flesh no and He is moved when we deny our flesh to come after Him through prayer and fasting.

One of the most powerful things I have learned about fasting is that it can change the direction of your life. We see this happen to the Apostle Paul in Acts 9. Acts 9:1–12 says, "During those days, Saul, full of angry threats and rage, wanted to murder the disciples of the Lord Jesus. So he went to ask the high priest and requested a letter of authorization he could take to the Jewish leaders in Damascus requesting their cooperation in finding and arresting...all of the believers...So he obtained the authorization and left for Damascus. Just outside the city, a brilliant light flashing from Heaven suddenly exploded all around him. Falling to the ground, he heard a booming voice say to him, "Saul, Saul, why are you persecuting me?" The men accompanying Saul were stunned and speechless, for they heard a heavenly voice but could see no one. Saul replied, "Who are you, Lord?" "I am Jesus, the Victorious, the one you are persecuting. Now, get up and go into the city, where you will be told what you are to do." Saul stood to his feet, and even though his eyes were open he could see nothing—he was blind. So the men had to take him by the hand and lead him into Damascus. For three days he didn't eat or drink and couldn't see a thing. Living in Damascus was a believer named Ananias. The Lord spoke to him in a vision, calling his name. "Ananias." "Yes, Lord," Ananias answered. The Lord said, "Go at once to the street called Abundance and look for a man from Tarsus named Saul. You will find him at Judah's house. While he was praying, he saw in a supernatural vision a man named Ananias coming to lay hands upon him to restore his sight."

At the beginning of this passage we find Saul full of anger and rage wanting to murder the disciples of Jesus. On his way to Damascus, Saul encounters Jesus and his life is changed forever. We see in verse 9 that Saul didn't eat or drink for three days, which meant he was fasting. Acts 9:18 says, All at once, the crusty substance that was over Saul's eyes disappeared and he could see perfectly. Immediately, he got up and was baptized. After eating a meal, his strength returned." So if his strength returned after he broke his fast, whose strength was Saul operating in for those 3 days? It was in God's strength. Paul would later write in 2 Corinthians 12:9, "And He said to me, 'My grace is sufficient for you, for My strength is made perfect in weakness.'"

This entire passage tells us so much about fasting. We see from this story of Saul's powerful conversion that fasting truly can change the entire direction of your life! During this one fast, Saul encountered Jesus, became a Christian, saw a vision and was baptized. Acts 9:20 tells us that, within the hour, Paul was in the synagogues, preaching about Jesus and proclaiming, "Jesus is the Son of God!" Saul's three-day fast changed his life, his nature, and his future. It changed who he spent his time with, and it even changed his name. Are you believing for something to change?

You can assess that same strength and power of God that Paul did as you fast and pray.

We also see the power of fasting to change a situation in the book of Daniel. Daniel knew the power of fasting. He begins in Daniel 1 by telling his flesh no. King Nebuchadnezzar of Babylon declared war on Jerusalem. He ordered his men to find some Israelites from the royal family and nobility—young men who were healthy and handsome, intelligent and well-educated, great prospects for leadership positions in the government to be brought to be trained for 3 years in his court. King Nebuchadnezzar planned to indoctrinate them in the Babylonian language and in their pagan practices. The king wanted these Israelite men to be served from the same menu as he was. He wanted them to be given the best food and the finest wine so that they would look and grow strong. However Daniel 1:8 says, "But Daniel purposed in his heart that he would not defile himself with the portion of the king's delicacies, nor with the wine which he drank; therefore he requested of the chief of the eunuchs that he might not defile himself." Daniel knew that his strength did not come from food but that it came from the Lord. This is why Daniel set himself apart in fasting because he knew that if he could remain consecrated to the Lord and tell his flesh no then he would be able to steward his time in Babylon righteously.

Daniel 1:14–20 says, "He (the king's steward) consented with them in this matter...and at the end of ten days their features appeared better and fatter in flesh than all the young men who ate the portion of the king's delicacies. Thus the steward took away their portion of delicacies and the wine that they were to drink and gave them vegetables. As for these four young men, God gave them knowledge and skill in all literature and wisdom; and Daniel had understanding in all visions and dreams. Now at the end of the days, when the king had said that they should be brought in, the chief of the eunuchs brought them in before Nebuchadnezzar. Then the king interviewed them, and among them all none was found like Daniel, Hananiah, Mishael, and Azariah; therefore they served before the king. And in all matters of wisdom *and* understanding about which the king examined them, he found them ten times better than all the magicians *and* astrologers who *were* in all his realm."

Daniel chose to eat vegetables and water instead of the king's delicacies. Daniel was given knowledge and skill and gifted with understanding, dreams, and visions. He and his friends even looked better than the others around them all because of their decision to fast! Whenever you fast you are setting yourself up for success. During a fast, you may even receive business ideas, knowledge, and greater wisdom from the Lord during that time. Why? Because, just as with Daniel, God honors and rewards us whenever we choose to set ourselves apart from the world's delicacies. Some of you may have prophetic dreams and visions that you do not understand. Try going on a fast and see how the Lord give you revelation and insight about them. Do you want the ability to understand your dreams and visions? Tell your flesh no, set yourself apart in fasting and see what breakthrough comes your way!

Daniel 10:10 tells us how Daniel fasted and prayed for breakthrough for 21 days. Again, during this time he only ate vegetables and ate no meat or delicacies. The Bible says that the angel of the Lord came to him and told him that God heard his prayer on the first day, but the battle had been raging with the Prince of Persia and he had been detained. I believe, like Daniel, there is a spirit of delay that can hold up things that you have been praying for. I believe the Lord is bringing breakthrough for every promise He has given you as you fast. Fasting breaks the spirit of delay. Don't lose hope during the delay. God hears every prayer! Hang on to every promise, declare God's Word over them said that they had explored the option of flying back to Dallas, but the plane didn't have enough fuel to make it back. Still after many hours, the lighting kept on and we could not taxi to the jet bridge. As time passed, people grew restless, hungry, tired, and cranky. We had been there for four hours. It was now the early morning hours that are still considered the middle of the night.

At the time, I was on a negative fast. Periodically, I will go on what I call a negative fast, where I do not allow myself to say anything negative. I do this to reset the words I allow to come out of my mouth. During this situation, I happened to be on one of my negative fasts. I was trying not to let any corrupt communication come out of my mouth. So, I sat mostly silently just thinking about how bad this situation was. I was thinking about the car we had rented to get us around Colorado on our trip. I remember realizing that at 4 am the desk where we could pick up our car would now be closed meaning we would have to find a different form of transportation to our hotel even if we did get off of the plane anytime soon. I remember thinking about how our schedule for the rest of the day would be totally disrupted because we would need to catch up on sleep, take time to make it back to the airport to pick up our rental car and spend time rescheduling what we had originally planned for the day. Delay after delay after delay was rolling around in my mind as we sat there, still in our plane seats, waiting.

Finally, at 4 am, the captain said, "We are cleared to taxi to the terminal." So with a plane full of elated passengers, the plane began moving forward toward the jet bridge. I expected to feel the plane rolling forward for at least several minutes. We moved this big 747 just barely twenty yards. This entire time I thought we were out in the middle of the tarmac, and actually, we were a few yards away. It was dark and we were tired. We didn't know we were so close. We were being beat up by hail and considered going back as lighting was all around. But breakthrough was only twenty yards away. Part of me is thankful that I did not know how close we were to the jet bridge or I probably would have jumped out of one the emergency exits!

I want to declare to you that you are on the edge of your breakthrough. You may not be able to see it but you are so close! Don't consider what's going on outside. Don't pay attention to the storm around you. It may be dark, you may be tired, but breakthrough is coming. Like Daniel, God heard you on the first day. Some things have been held up in air traffic control in the heavenlies but fasting can break the spirit of delay!

and do not give in to discouragement. Just like Daniel, your breakthrough can be unlocked as you continue in fasting and prayer.

The story of Daniel reminds me of a time I was only twenty yards away from breakthrough without knowing it. We were on board a beautiful 747 American Airlines, flight 575, nonstop service from Dallas to Colorado Springs. We had just landed when a large storm came off the beautiful Rocky Mountains. There was thunder, lightning and hail coming down all around us as we sat on the landing strip. Our pilot came over the intercom to let us know that air traffic control would not allow us to move into the terminal. Because of the storm, we could not taxi to the jet bridge because the ground crew could not come out due to the lightning. Every thirty to sixty minutes—for hours—the captain would report what the air traffic controller said. "We are delayed. We are going to be here for a while."

Meanwhile, we were still sitting right where we landed, still stuck inside the plane. Our plane was being hit with large hail. It sounded as if someone was throwing quarters at a tin can. The storm continued outside with rolling thunder, loud crashes of lightning and lots of rain. After several more hours, the captain

God is on your side for breakthrough. Whatever obstacles that have had you confined can be conquered by denying your flesh. As you access the breakthrough made available to you through fasting and prayer, those forces that have kept you back from the promises that God has given to you will no longer be able to hold you back. He's ready to bring you through those places you've been constantly ensnared. The Lord wants to set you free from the things that have constricted and limited you. God's desire is to bring you into a land of victory, a land of breakthrough. You can get on the fast track to your promises and the breakthrough God has for you by fasting!

Chapter 6

THOSE WHO FASTED

In this chapter, I want to discuss some of the people in scripture who used the power of fasting to reach their breakthrough. The first one that comes to mind is from one of my favorite scriptures which is 2 Samuel 5:20 which says, "So David went to Baal Perazim, and David defeated them there; and he said, "The Lord has broken through my enemies before me, like a breakthrough of water." Another translation calls the Lord hear, "The Lord of the breakthrough". Some of you have known God as Father, friend, or Savior. But has God become the Lord of the breakthrough in your life? There is so much power in fasting to release breakthrough. I know we've discussed this many times so far, but if you could only see what's on the other side of your decision to fast you would say yes to it!

When I think about a person who truly tapped into the power of acting on a prophetic word from God by committing to fast and pray, I think about Esther. Esther was just a simple Jewish girl who ended up in the king's palace. Esther found herself in possession of the king's favor when she and her people needed it the most. Esther was unafraid to cry out to God to save her and her people. She recognized the significance of her time and where she found herself. Esther 3:8–11 says, Then Haman said to King Ahasuerus, "There is a certain people scattered and dispersed among the people in all the provinces of your kingdom; their laws are different from all other people's, and they do not keep the king's laws. Therefore it is not fitting for the king to let them remain. If it pleases the king, let a decree be written that they be destroyed, and I will pay ten thousand talents of silver into the hands of those who do the work, to bring it into the king's treasuries." So the king took his signet ring from his hand and gave it to Haman, the son of Hammedatha the Agagite, the enemy of the Jews. And the king said to Haman, "The money and the people are given to you, to do with them as seems good to you."

Esther and her people were in danger of utter destruction if she did not do something, if God did not come through for them. So Esther recognizes the significance of this moment and chooses to fast. Esther 4:1–3,13–17 says, "When Mordecai learned all that had happened he tore his clothes and put on sackcloth and ashes, and went out into the midst of the city. He cried out with a loud and bitter cry. He went as far as the front of the king's gate, for no one might enter the king's gate clothed with sackcloth. And in every province where the king's command and decree arrived, there was great mourning among the Jews, with fasting, weeping, and wailing; and many lay in sackcloth and ashes. And Mordecai told them to answer Esther: "Do not think in your heart that you will escape in the king's palace any more than all the other Jews. For if you remain completely silent at this time, relief and deliverance will arise for the Jews from another place, but you and your father's house will perish. Yet who knows whether you have come to the kingdom for such a time as this?" Then Esther told them to reply to Mordecai: "Go, gather all the Jews who are present in Shushan, and fast for me; neither eat nor drink for three days, night or day. My maids and I will fast likewise. And so I will go to the king, which is against the law; and if I perish, I perish!" So Mordecai went his way and did according to all that Esther commanded him."

Esther calls a fast and moves forward, not fearing what may happen if she does obey God. This tells me she feared more what would happen if she did not obey the Lord. Do we fear the Lord like Esther did? Are we willing to fast so that others can be saved? Are we willing to say, "If I perish, I perish but I'm not going down without fighting through prayer and fasting?"

I could not write a book about fasting for breakthrough without looking at the story of Jehoshaphat in 2 Chronicles 20. 2 Chronicles 20:1-4 says, "It happened after this that the people of Moab with the people of Ammon, and others with them besides the Ammonites, came to battle against Jehoshaphat. Then some came and told Jehoshaphat, saying, "A great multitude is coming against you from beyond the sea, And Jehoshaphat feared, and set himself to seek the Lord, and proclaimed a fast throughout all Judah. So Judah gathered together to ask help from the Lord; and from all the cities of Judah they came to seek the Lord." When Jehoshaphat found that he and his men were surrounded by their enemies, he did not cower in fear. He did not retreat. Instead, Jehoshaphat recognized where His victory must come from. He knew that he and his men could not defeat the enemy armies without God fighting for them. So Jehoshaphat did the wisest thing that any of us can do; he cried out to God and called a fast. How many times do we retreat instead of fasting and pursuing our victory? How many times have we lost a battle by trying to win it in our own strength? We must take this truth from Jehoshaphat: fasting is the key to victory over the enemy.

2 Chronicles 20:5–18 says, Then Jehoshaphat stood in the assembly of Judah and Jerusalem, in the house of the Lord, before the new court, and said: "O Lord God of our fathers, are You not God in Heaven, and do You not rule over all the kingdoms of the nations, and in Your hand is there not power and might, so that no one is able to withstand You? Here they are, rewarding us by coming to throw us out of Your possession which You have given us to inherit. O our God, will You not judge them? For we have no power against this great multitude that is coming against us; nor do we know what to do, but our eyes are upon You." Now all Judah, with their little ones, their wives, and their children, stood before the Lord. You will not need to fight in this battle. Position yourselves, stand still and see the salvation of the Lord, who is with you, O Judah and Jerusalem!' Do not fear or be dismayed; tomorrow go out against them, for the Lord is with you." And Jehoshaphat bowed his head with his face to the ground, and all Judah and the inhabitants of Jerusalem bowed before the Lord, worshiping the Lord." Jehoshaphat fasted and prayed, along with his men, and they received a prophetic promise from the

Lord about the battle they were to fight. The word of the Lord to them was that they needed only to be still, because the Lord would fight this battle for them. When we fast and when we pray, God fights our battles for us. The most powerful thing you can do to gain victory over the enemy is to seek the Lord in humility by fasting and praying.

2 Chronicles 20:20–25 says, "So they rose early in the morning and went out into the Wilderness of Tekoa; and as they went out, Jehoshaphat stood and said, "Hear me, O Judah and you inhabitants of Jerusalem: Believe in the Lord your God, and you shall be established; believe His prophets, and you shall prosper." And when he had consulted with the people, he appointed those who should sing to the Lord, and who should praise the beauty of holiness, as they went out before the army and were saying: "Praise the Lord, for His mercy endures forever." Now when they began to sing and to praise, the Lord set ambushes against the people of Ammon, Moab, and Mount Seir, who had come against Judah; and they were defeated. For the people of Ammon and Moab stood up against the inhabitants of Mount Seir to utterly kill and destroy them. And when they had made an end of the inhabitants of Seir, they helped to destroy one another. So when Judah came to a place

overlooking the wilderness, they looked toward the multitude; and there were their dead bodies, fallen on the earth. No one had escaped. When Jehoshaphat and his people came to take away their spoil, they found among them an abundance of valuables on the dead bodies, and precious jewelry, which they stripped off for themselves, more than they could carry away; and they were three days gathering the spoil because there was so much." There are spoils of the enemy waiting for you on the other side of your commitment to fast and pray! What victory are you missing out on because you haven't fasted. When God fights our battles, we gain complete victory and walk away with the spoils of the enemy. God is enthroned on our praises, and when our praises are backed by the power of fasting and prayer, nothing can stop us. God wins every single battle He fights, so we should let Him fight all our battles.

Another important time in scripture where fasting unlocked breakthrough was in the book of Acts. In Acts 13, believers were often sent out and commissioned after times of fasting and prayer. A greater dimension of your purpose and destiny can be unlocked in a season of consecration and fasting. Acts 13:2–3 says, "As they ministered to the Lord and fasted, the Holy Spirit said, 'Now separate to Me Barnabas and Saul for the work to which I have called them.' Then, having fasted and prayed, and laid hands on them, they sent them away." The words "have called" here mean "to summon to oneself." God was calling Barnabas and Saul to Himself because of their obedience in fasting and prayer. If these men had not fasted it is possible that the Lord would have chosen other men for this Kingdom assignment. God is looking for those who He can use to advance His Kingdom. Why does fasting prepare you to be used by God? A degree of humility comes with fasting that will propel us into purpose. Acts 14:22–23 says, "Strengthening the souls of the disciples, exhorting them to continue in the faith, and saying, 'We must through many tribulations enter the Kingdom of God.' So when they had appointed elders in every church, and prayed with fasting, they commended them to the Lord in whom they had believed." Both "strengthening" and "confirming" in these verses mean to give them something to lean on or hold on to. God was strengthening them to do His will by the means of fasting and prayer. Fasting draws us closer to God and prepares us for activity with God. Fasting propels us forward into our destiny.

As my wife, Autumn discussed in Chapter 5, Daniel was one in scripture that tapped into the power of fasting and prayer to release breakthrough. In Daniel

10, we see this power of fasting to bring breakthrough. Daniel 10:2–3,12–13 says, "In those days I, Daniel, was mourning three full weeks. I ate no pleasant food, no meat or wine came into my mouth, nor did I anoint myself at all, till three whole weeks were fulfilled. Then he said to me, "Do not fear, Daniel, for from the first day that you set your heart to understand, and to humble yourself before your God, your words were heard; and I have come because of your words. But the prince of the kingdom of Persia withstood me twenty-one days; and behold, Michael, one of the chief princes, came to help me, for I had been left alone there with the kings of Persia." Daniel's fast broke the stronghold of principality of Persia and released the archangel Michael. There are some stronghold that can only be taken down by fasting and prayer. Fasting helps break strongholds and defeat the power of the enemy over individuals, situations and even nations!

We obviously cannot look at those who fasted in scripture without talking about Jesus! Luke 4:14 says, "Then Jesus returned in the power of the Spirit to Galilee, and news of Him went out through all the surrounding region. And He taught in their synagogues, being glorified by all." A specific power and authority can only come to you from fasting. To reach the deep things of God, we must go through wilderness and cave seasons. After He was baptized, the Holy Spirit drove Jesus into the wilderness to fast and to be tested. Matthew 4:1–2 says, "Then Jesus was led up by the Spirit into the wilderness to be tempted by the devil. And after fasting forty days and forty nights, he was hungry." The process takes you to the promise. If Jesus needed to be led away into the wilderness of fasting, then we must also. The process gives you the ability to handle what God has called you to do.

During some seasons, you will be led by the Spirit into the wilderness to fast. God always does this for a reason. Jesus died on the cross in complete brokenness for us. God loves brokenness. When we are completely broken to our will, God can then use us to complete our God assignment. Fasting brings us into a place of brokenness. After Jesus had fasted for forty days, He started his earthly ministry. Fasting is effective when you're desperate for God to move in a situation or if you want a deeper connection with Him. We fast to spend more time with Him.

During seasons of fasting, you will gain key wisdom and insight for the future. Seasons of fasting can erase insecurity and fear from your life. These times are to refresh you with the Lord and to bring you back to your identity as a true son or daughter of God. Luke 9:23 says, "Jesus said 'If anyone desires to come after Me, let him deny himself, and take up his cross daily, and follow Me.'" The bottom line of fasting is denying ourselves so that we can have more of God and become more like Him.

Chapter 7

ACCELERATE YOUR BREAKTHROUGH

Have you ever felt like every single time you get ready to advance you begin to hit roadblocks? Maybe you feel as if you are about to run the hundred-yard dash, but when the gun goes off, it turns into the hundred-and-ten-yard dash—with hurdles! Like the children of Israel, it might seem as if you were only supposed to go on an eleven-day journey, but it has been forty years and you are still waiting outside the promised land.

Breakthrough has been a kind of buzz word in church culture for quite some time. Many messages have been preached and many songs have been written about breakthrough. Honestly, how many conferences or gatherings have you been to that were titled "Breakthrough"? Probably many. But what is breakthrough really?

The word breakthrough means "a dramatic and important change, discovery or development." When we are in need of a breakthrough, we are bound by something or something is blocking our way forward. If you have walked with God for any amount of time, you have probably learned that breakthrough will be something you need over and over again. As a believer, breakthrough is often not just a one-time event but it can become a lifestyle. Jesus demonstrated this in His life as He was constantly advancing the Kingdom of God the enemy would always try to stop Him. One thing we can be sure of is that the enemy will never let us take any territory without a fight.

When we are waiting for God to break through for us, we like to believe that our breakthrough will come suddenly. We hope that our breakthrough will come the first time we pray or answer an altar call for it. I have personally had many breakthrough encounters that came that easily and suddenly. However, I have also believed and contended for a breakthrough for a long time before I experienced it. We can and will receive breakthrough in numerous ways. Sometimes our breakthroughs come suddenly. However, most of the time we must fight in order to get our breakthrough.

As we have discussed throughout this book, there is a way to fast track or accelerate your breakthrough through prayer and fasting. If we want to accelerate our breakthrough, we must wield the spiritual weapons of fasting and prayer against the enemy who is constantly trying to delay us. However, we must be wise in our warfare to ensure that we are always operating in the Spirit of God. Do not fret and work yourself up so much waiting on your breakthrough that when it finally happens, you are too worn out to function effectively in it. The enemy will always try to wear you out and tire you out with a steady stream of intense warfare whenever he senses you are nearing breakthrough. You must always remember to not look at where you are but rather at where you are going. Never focus on the area in which you need breakthrough but choose instead to hone in on the promises God has made to you. Keep moving forward with the Lord with clarity, dogged determination, and faith. Each obstacle is simply a hurdle put in your way to slow you down or distract you. Don't let it!

Breakthrough has been a kind of buzz word in church culture for quite some time. Many messages have been preached and many songs have been written about breakthrough. Honestly, how many conferences or gatherings have you been to that were titled "Breakthrough"? Probably many. But what is breakthrough really?

The word breakthrough means "a dramatic and important change, discovery or development." When we are in need of a breakthrough, we are bound by something or something is blocking our way forward. If you have walked with God for any amount of time, you have probably learned that breakthrough will be something you need over and over again. As a believer, breakthrough is often not just a one-time event but it can become a lifestyle. Jesus demonstrated this in His life as He was constantly advancing the Kingdom of God the enemy would always try to stop Him. One thing we can be sure of is that the enemy will never let us take any territory without a fight. Fasting helps release the breaker anointing! An anointing is coming to the church to break strongholds over families and regions. Fasting will help you break any limitations you may have. God's will is for every believer to live a victorious life. Pray and fast and receive all that God has for you. Settle for nothing less. Fasting gives you clear insight on how to declare and decree over your life and family.

When times of trouble hit, remember that God uses such seasons to stretch, prepare, and train you as an equipped soldier. You do not become stronger in the good times. You only become stronger by enduring and persevering through times of adversity. Always keep in mind that the devil never goes to battle where there are no spoils. When you find your true identity in God and have come into the awareness of your God-given purpose and destiny, the enemy will launch his strongest and most vehement attacks. He does not want the children of God to understand or walk in the full measure of their God-given authority and power. This is why it is important to remember that we, as children of God, have power to win every battle. When my son Ezra was six, he would say every night when he prayed, "We win every time with God, and the devil loses every battle every time."

My Apostle, Ken Malone shares a story about one of his grandchildren calling the enemy, "the forever loser" because God wins every time! I absolutely love that. Some of the ways the Bible refers to the forever loser are the enemy, the thief, and the devil. Whatever we call him, he is always trying to kill, abort, destroy, intimidate, or frustrate everything you try to do for God. John 10:10 says, "The thief comes to kill, steal, and destroy. But I have come to give you life and life more abundantly."

Now let's look at the four keywords in John 10:10. The word "kill" means to cause death to a person or a living thing. When you receive a word straight from the Lord or a prophetic word, that word is alive, but the enemy wants to kill it. The word "steal" means to take something without permission with the intention of never returning it. The thief has no right to take anything from you. When he takes something from you, you have to tell your heavenly Father and go get it back. The word "destroy" means to put an end to the existence of something or to cause ruin physically, emotionally, or spiritually. The devil wants to bring destruction in every area of your life, especially to all your relationships and existing projects. The main problem for him, though, is that his words have no power over that which God has called, blessed, and spoken favor and increase into. God's word trumps the devil's word 100 percent of the time.

Now, let's get to the word I like the best in this particular scripture, and that is the word abundantly. The word "abundantly" means in large, plenty, or extreme quantities. So every area the devil tries to kill, steal, and destroy are the exact same areas where God wants to restore and bring large quantities of overflow. God wants to give us plenty in every area we need it and add extreme measures of His blessings to our lives. I will believe the report of the Lord all the days of my life. Far too many people have wasted enough of their lives and time worrying about the attacks, schemes, and plans of the devil when God has an extremely abundant life, full of breakthrough, waiting for them. Now is the time for you to start walking in the fullness of the powerful and heavily anointed words God has spoken over your life.

When the Israelites entered the promised land, they didn't take natural ownership overnight. They had to go through a process. Some battles take a while. The greatest battle you will ever fight will have a lot of on-the-job training. Stay near to God, for He will lead you through. Romans 8:31 says, "What then shall we say to these things? If God is for us, who can be against us?" When you are confident that God is on your side, you will surely have victory. Half the battle is knowing that God is with us and for us. Our confidence in God's delivering power is strengthened when we draw near to him through prayer and fasting. 1 John 4:4 says, "You are of God, little children, and have overcome them, because He who is in you is greater than he who is in the world." The God in you is greater than the enemy and anything the enemy may try to throw at you. Don't be worried or afraid; you can overcome the enemy because Jesus has already overcome him. 2 Timothy 1:7 says, "For God has not given us a spirit of fear, but of power and of love and of a sound mind. Since God has already given us power, love and a sound mind." If we aren't walking in these things, we need to fast and break whatever cycle or stronghold is binding us up. Fear and insecurity can become a crippling spirit to many. These spirits and mindsets keep people from moving forward.

If you want a better tomorrow, start fasting today. What you do today determines your tomorrow. James 1:22 says, "But be doers of the word, and not hearers only, deceiving yourselves." So many people feel stuck in life or feel as if things are mundane or complacent. Well, fast and break out of that cycle. If you want all that God has for you, do all that God says to do.

As I was praying about a speaking engagement on breakthrough one day, the Lord gave me this paragraph: "Sometimes the breakthrough is simply the end of the process that God was using to take you toward a certain destination. You must learn to endure and allow the process to teach and grow you. Do not sit around and cry and complain, or you will not learn what you desperately need to for your next assignment. If you do not break, you will have your breakthrough. God will use the hard times to prepare you. These times will be full of pressure, but you will come out properly equipped for your next season. Take courage—your breakthrough is at hand!"

In life, the four Ts will come for you: test, trials, temptations, and tribulations. James 1:2-4 says, "My fellow believers, when it seems as though you are facing nothing but difficulties, see it as an invaluable opportunity to experience the greatest joy that you can! For you know that when your faith is tested it stirs up in you the power of endurance. And then as your endurance grows even stronger, it will release perfection into every part of your being until there is nothing missing and nothing lacking." Wow! God's perspective on the difficult seasons of our lives is revolutionary. What could the times of testing and trials produce in us if we say them as opportunities instead of defeat? If we are going to do anything great for God, we must have endurance and perseverance. My friends, we do not learn or grow the most in the mountain top, victorious seasons. Instead we experience the most transformation in the hard times.

If we could learn to embrace our moments of warfare and the hard times, we would see that the Lord does His best work when we are in trouble. When these things occur, learn to rejoice. It takes the wind out of the enemy's sails. Choose instead to remain laser-focused on God, and He will get you through every one of these tests, trials, and tribulations. The constant attacks can either advance us or detour us. We need to understand that advancement in the Kingdom of God usually comes after the enemy's attacks. The harsher the attack, the greater the Kingdom advancement.

Psalm 46:1 tells us that "God is our refuge and strength; a very present help in times of trouble." Our daily relationship with the Lord will establish in us a confident faith and trust in the Lord. So much so that whenever hard times come, we will know that He is the good shepherd and a safe place of refuge for us. As such, we can rest assured that no strategic attack of the enemy will ever overtake us. Isaiah 54:17 says, "No weapon formed against you shall prosper, and every tongue which rises against you in judgment You shall condemn. This is the heritage of the servants of the Lord, and their righteousness is from Me," Says the Lord. This scripture does not say that a weapon would never form against you. It only says that any weapon that is formed against you will not prosper.

Whenever we need breakthrough, we must remember that the attack or the warfare we are presently going through is only temporary. 1 Corinthians 10:13 states,

"No temptation has overtaken you except such as is common to man; but God is faithful, who will not allow you to be tempted beyond what you are able, but with the temptation will also make the way of escape, that you may be able to bear it." God will never let anything you face to completely overtake you. God is your way of escape and your defender. Often God will use our opposition in order to get us into proper position for whatever He has for us. This is why you should never despise your need for breakthrough, lean into the Lord and trust that He will come through for you every single time.

The majority of things, if not all, I have created or achieved in my life were birthed out of a fast. There is something so powerful about the clarity that comes from fasting. Fasting helps us to keep our focus on God when we encounter difficulties. When we fast, our expectations and our faith for the Lord to move on our behalf rise. Psalm 37:34 says, "So don't be impatient for the Lord to act; keep moving forward steadily in his ways, and he will exalt you at the right time. And when he does, you will possess every promise, including your full inheritance. You'll watch with your own eyes and see the wicked lose everything." 2 Chronicles 16:9 says, "For the eyes of the Lord run to and fro throughout the whole earth, to show Himself strong on behalf of those whose heart is loyal to Him." God is looking for somebody just like you. The Lord has so many plans and dreams for the earth. He is just looking for someone in whom He can plant a seed of destiny so deep into the fertile ground of their willing and surrendered heart that it produces powerful fruit for His Kingdom. The eyes of the Lord are looking over all the earth to find that one person, group of people, ministry, church, or business owner whose heart is completely His. Whenever God places a powerful destiny into somebody in seed form, those with hearts completely loyal to Him are able to fulfill it to the fullest possible measure. The reason for this is because when a seed is planted in the natural, a farmer must water, fertilize, and tend to the soil. He must be diligent to keep the animals and birds away from the seed, pull surrounding weeds up, and take good care of the ground. In the same way, the Spirit of the Lord is looking for someone who will keep their life on the altar of God, someone who will live their life as a living sacrifice unto God so that the plans and destiny He has for them will be fulfilled.

The Word says that God will show Himself strong on your behalf, which means He will fight your battles for you and win your wars. He will commission angels of mercy, grace, and power to encamp all around you. He will bring finances and ample resources to fund your destiny. He will cause people to come alongside you and help steward the call He has placed on your life. God's eyes are running all over the earth, looking for that one person who is living their life in His presence, who's number one desire is to seek and find Him on a daily basis. The Lord knows that He can entrust this person with a great destiny because they will take the steps necessary each day to accomplish all He has placed on their heart. You may be called to be a stay-at-home mom and raise three world changers, you may be a high school coach, nurse, teacher, or intercessor. No matter what path you have been called to walk, keep your eyes steadfastly on the Lord, and as you do, your eyes will lock, and your gaze will meet His. From this posture of intimacy, the Lord will reveal a greater purpose and destiny to you and show Himself strong on your behalf.

Those found in the wilderness of fasting will usher in the next great move of God. If you have found yourself paralyzed by delay and are longing for your breakthrough, you now have the keys you need to step into all that God has for you. Go forth and step into the fullness of God. Use the powerful weapon of fasting and know that your breakthrough is just around the corner. Fasting is the fast track to breakthrough!

ABOUT THE AUTHORS

Joe Joe and Autumn Dawson are the Founders and Apostolic Oversight of ROAR Church Texarkana. Their desire is to see every believer fulfill their God-given destiny and live life to the fullest in God. The Dawsons travel the nation with a message of personal revival, freedom, purpose and destiny. They reside in Texarkana, Texas with their 3 children: Malachi, Judah & Ezra.

CONNECT WITH JOE JOE

JOE JOE DAWSON MINISTRIES

- **JOE JOE DAWSON**
  FACEBOOK

- **@JOE_JOE_DAWSONTXK**
  INSTAGRAM

- **JOE JOE DAWSON**
  YOUTUBE

- **JOEJOEDAWSON.NET**
  WEBSITE